INSTRUMENTS

FOLK AND COUNTRY

Roger Thomas

Heinemann
LIBRARY

First published in Great Britain by Heinemann Library
Halley Court, Jordan Hill, Oxford OX2 8EJ
a division of Reed Educational and Professional Publishing Ltd.
Heinemann is a registered trademark of Reed Educational and Professional Publishing Ltd.

OXFORD FLORENCE PRAGUE MADRID ATHENS
MELBOURNE AUCKLAND KUALA LUMPUR SINGAPORE TOKYO
IBADAN NAIROBI KAMPALA JOHANNESBURG GABORONE
PORTSMOUTH NH (USA) CHICAGO MEXICO CITY SAO PAULO

Designed by Susan Clarke
Printed in Hong Kong

03 02 01 00 99
10 9 8 7 6 5 4 3 2 1

ISBN 0 431 08815 2

British Library Cataloguing in Publication Data

Thomas, Roger
Folk & country. – (Instruments in music)
1.Folk music – Juvenile literature 2.Country music – Juvenile literature
I.Title
781.4'162

This book is also available in hardback (ISBN 0 431 08807 1)

Acknowledgements
The Publishers would like to thank the following for permission to reproduce photographs: Dat's Jazz Picture Library, pp.4, 11, pp.5, 15 (Robin Somes); Trevor Clifford, pp.8, 9, 25 (Derek Jolly. p.25 Tea-chest made and supplied by Steve Dwyer); Liz Eddison/Hobgoblin Music. pp.6, 7, 10, 12, 16, 18, 20, 24, 26; Hutchison Library, p.14; Redferns, pp.22, 23, p.13 (Patrick Ford), pp.17, 27 (Leon Morris), p.19 (Odile Noel), p.21 (Brian Shuel); Sylvia Pitcher Photo Library, p.29, p.28 (Susan Francis).

Cover photograph: PhotoEdit/Jeff Greenberg

Our thanks to Betty Root for her comments in the preparation of this book.

Every effort has been made to contact copyright holders of any material reproduced in this book. Any omissions will be rectified in subsequent printings if notice is given to the Publisher.

CONTENTS

Some words are shown in bold, **like this**. You can find out what they mean by looking in the Glossary.

INTRODUCTION

This book is about the many instruments used in folk and country music. Folk music really means any music written and played by ordinary people who may not be professional musicians. People have always done this, so it is a music which is thousands of years old. However, it is most often thought of as traditional music played mainly on **acoustic** instruments. It often includes singing.

A folk group

An American country band

Country music is a bit like folk music but it was started in one country – the USA – about a hundred years ago. The music is a mixture of folk music with jazz and blues music. It uses some of the same instruments as folk music.

THE ACOUSTIC GUITAR AND ACOUSTIC BASS GUITAR

Acoustic guitars in folk and country music are usually large and have six steel strings. This gives them a loud, bright sound. Singers often play acoustic guitars while they sing.

Acoustic guitars are very important instruments in folk and country music

acoustic bass guitar

acoustic guitar

One of these musicians is playing an acoustic guitar and the other an acoustic bass guitar

The strings on an acoustic guitar are strummed or plucked with the player's fingernails or with a **plectrum**. The acoustic bass guitar plays lower **notes** than the acoustic guitar. It has four thick strings which are plucked with the fingers or with a plectrum. The acoustic bass has a warm, deep sound.

ELECTRIC GUITARS

The steel guitar is a special **electric** guitar which is played flat on a stand or on the player's lap. The player uses a **plectrum** to pluck the strings, and changes the **notes** with a metal rod called a steel. The steel is moved along the strings to give the notes a sliding sound. The instrument must be played through an **amplifier**.

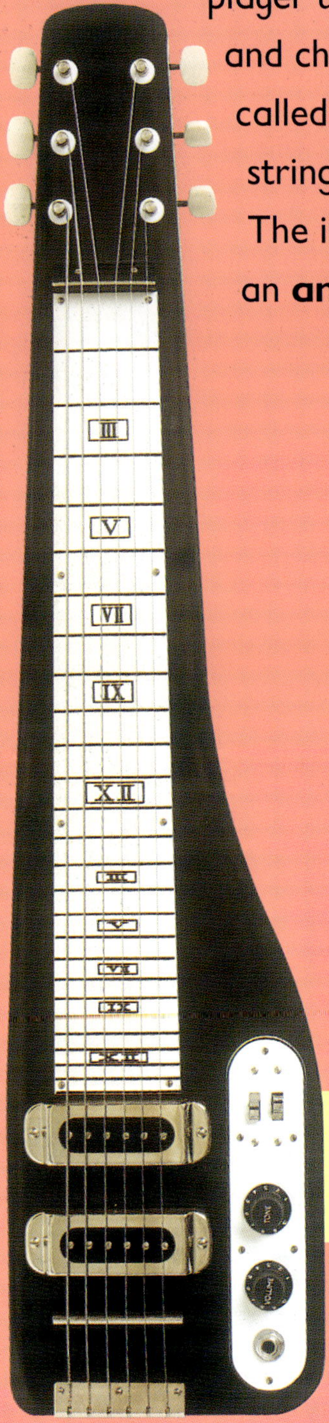

The steel guitar is often used in country music

This musician is playing a steel guitar

Ordinary electric guitars and bass guitars are also used in country music. They must be played through amplifiers. Country guitarists sometimes choose to play semi-**acoustic** guitars. This type is played through an amplifier but has a hollow body which makes the sound smoother and gentler.

THE BANJO

The banjo was developed from string instruments brought to the USA from Africa over two hundred years ago. It has a set of strings which are plucked by the player's fingers or with a **plectrum**. The **notes** are changed by pressing the strings onto thin metal rods called **frets** on the instrument's **neck**, like a guitar.

The banjo is a very important instrument in folk and country music

This musician is playing a five-string banjo

There are many different kinds of banjo. The five-string type is the one most often used in folk and country music. Others include the four-string banjo and the much smaller four-string ukelele banjo.

THE MANDOLIN, MANDOLA AND BOUZOUKI

The mandolin is a small string instrument with a high, bright sound. The mandola is like a mandolin but plays lower **notes**. Both these instruments were invented in Europe centuries ago. At that time these instruments had round backs. The ones used in modern folk music usually have flat backs which makes them easier to hold and to play.

These instruments all have thin steel strings. This gives them a bright, tinkling sound

This musician is playing a mandola

The bouzouki is like a mandolin but with a long **neck**. It was invented in Greece where it became popular in the 1920s but it is now used in the folk music of many countries, including Ireland. The long steel strings of the bouzouki give it a bright, twangy sound.

THE FIDDLE AND HURDY-GURDY

The fiddle is played in both folk and country music. It is the same instrument as the violin which is used in classical music. It makes a sound when the player strokes the strings with a **bow** covered in sticky **rosin**. The player changes the **notes** by pressing the strings against the **neck** of the instrument. The fiddle has a high, clear sound that is easy to hear, which is why it is often played in **folk dance** music.

The fiddle is another name for the violin

The hurdy-gurdy is played in folk music

The hurdy-gurdy makes a sound when the player turns a handle which rubs a wheel against the strings. The player changes the notes by pressing **keys** on the instrument. The hurdy-gurdy will keep playing a note for as long as the player turns the handle. It has a sharp, hard tone.

THE MELODEON, CONCERTINA AND ACCORDION

The melodeon, concertina and accordion are used in many kinds of folk and country music. They are played by squeezing and stretching the **bellows** in the middle of the instrument. The bellows push air against metal **reeds** which then make a sound. The player changes the **notes** by pressing buttons or **keys** at the ends of the instrument.

melodeon

concertina

These instruments all work in the same way

accordion

This musician is playing a melodeon

The concertina is the smallest of these instruments and has buttons for changing the notes at both ends, like the melodeon. The accordion has keys like a piano which are usually at one end but can be at both.

DRUMS AND PERCUSSION IN FOLK MUSIC

Many different kinds of drums and **percussion** instruments are used in folk music all over the world. There are drums which are played with the hands or sticks. There are also lots of rattling, clapping, jingling and ringing instruments such as bells, triangles, **bones** and tambourines.

All these percussion instruments can be used in folk music

This musician is playing a bodhran, which is an Irish folk drum

Often folk percussion instruments from different parts of the world will look and work very like each other. For example, there are Irish, Indian and Native American drums which are very alike.

FOLK FLUTES AND PIPES

The penny whistle (also called a flageolet) is made of metal or wood. The player blows into a **mouthpiece** and changes the **notes** by covering and uncovering holes on the instrument. The ocarina works in the same way but has a round shape. It is usually made of **pottery**. Flutes and fifes are played by blowing across the mouthpiece instead of straight into it.

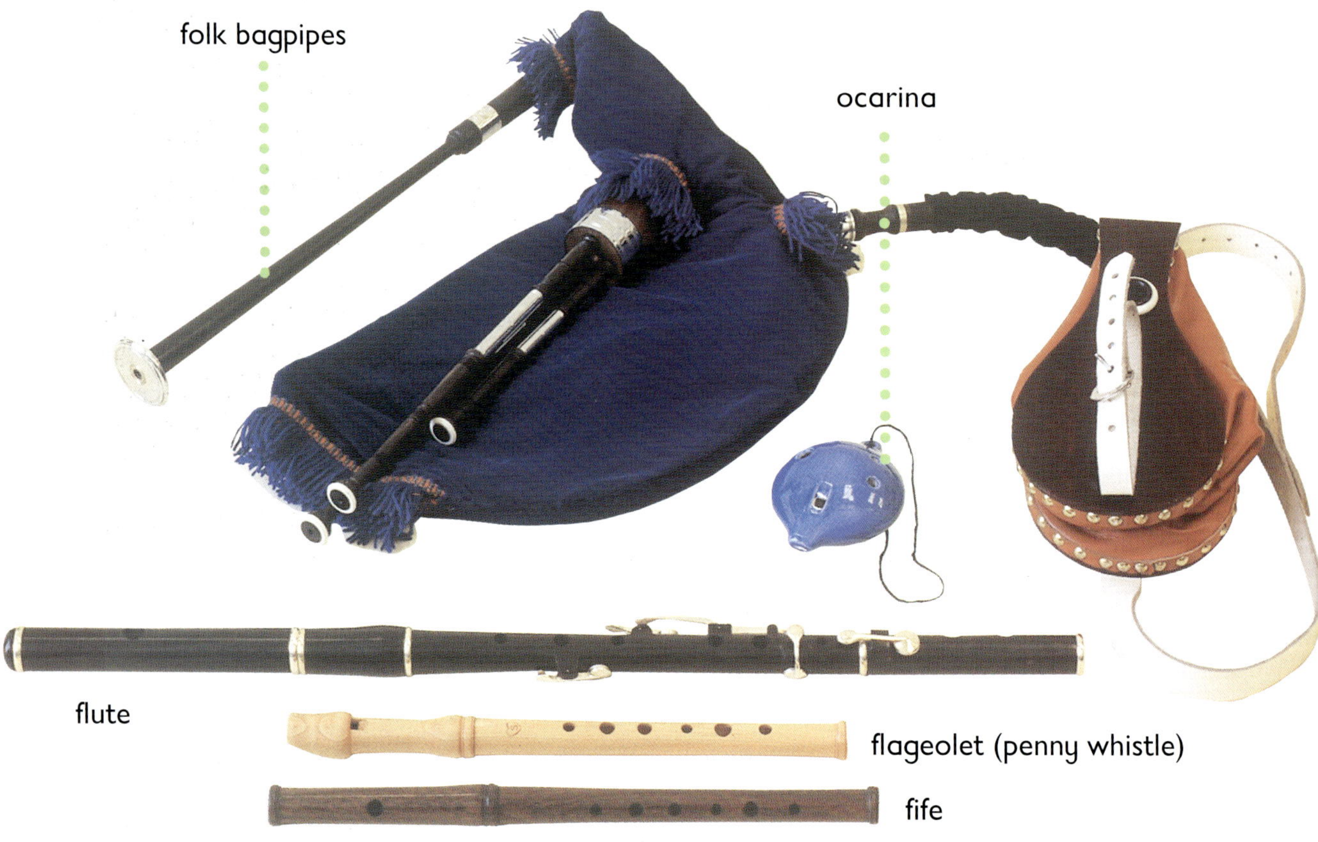

There are many kinds of folk wind instruments

This musician is playing a set of folk bagpipes

Folk bagpipes are a set of pipes with **reeds** inside. They make a sound when the player squeezes a set of **bellows** which push air into a bag. The air then goes from the bag into the pipes. The player changes the notes by covering and uncovering holes on one of the pipes.

SINGING IN COUNTRY AND FOLK MUSIC

Singing is perhaps more important in folk and country music than any instrument. The words in country and folks songs often tell a story or describe the singer's feelings. This means that the words and music are often simple and clear.

This singer is singing a country song

This is a folk singer

Folk songs can be sung **solo** or in a group with other voices. Solo folk singers will often also play an instrument such as a guitar while they sing. Folk groups will usually sing as well as play instruments. Country singers usually perform with a group.

SMALL AND HOME-MADE INSTRUMENTS

Small and home-made instruments are important in folk music because they are cheap and easy to carry and play. This means that many people can enjoy making music. The kazoo buzzes when the player hums into it. The Jew's harp is held against the player's teeth and makes a twanging sound when plucked. The Swanee whistle makes a sliding whistle sound. The harmonica has metal **reeds** which make a sound when the player blows into the instrument.

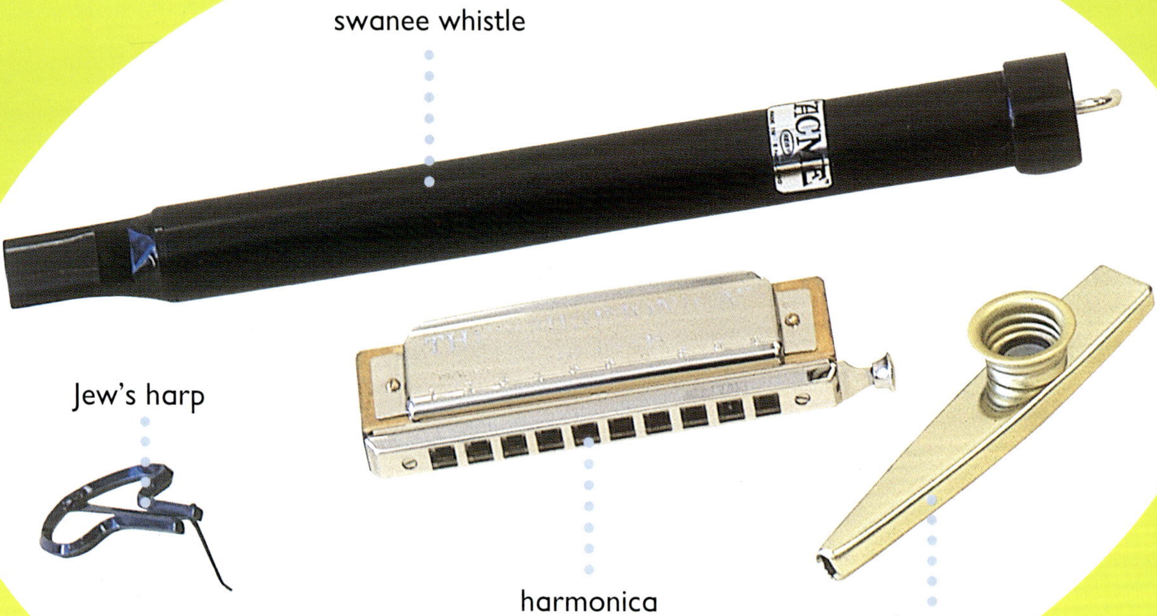

Small instruments like these are sometimes used in folk and country music

All these instruments are used in folk music but they are made from things once used in everyday life

The tea-chest bass is made from a tea-chest, a broom handle and a piece of string which the player plucks to make the **notes**. The jug is used as a wind instrument. The player blows across the opening of the jug to make a low note. The spoons are held in the player's hand and clapped together. The **washboard** is scraped to make a clattering sound.The lagerphone is made of bottle tops and is shaken or hit with a stick.

FOLK HARPS

Harps are used in folk music all over the world. They come in hundreds of different shapes and sizes. They are used as **solo** instruments and in groups with other instruments. Folk harps are usually made of wood. They have a set of strings which are stretched across a frame. The strings are fixed onto a hollow box at one end. This makes the sound louder.

This is a folk harp

This folk harpist is playing solo

The player plucks the strings of the harp with his or her fingers. The harp has a soft, delicate sound. There is usually no way of changing the **notes** the strings make on a folk harp. For this reason there is a string for every single note the instrument has to play.

THE DULCIMER AND AUTOHARP

The dulcimer and autoharp are string instruments used in folk music. The autoharp is used in country music as well. It is played by strumming or plucking the strings. The player changes the **notes** by pressing buttons on the instrument. The buttons push soft pads onto the strings which the player does not want to sound. The autoharp has a lively, clear sound.

This musician is playing an autoharp

This musician is playing a dulcimer

The dulcimer is played by hitting the strings with small **hammers** held in the player's hands, or by strumming them with a **plectrum**. The strings make different notes. The dulcimer has a quiet, jangly sound.

GLOSSARY

acoustic an instrument which can work without an amplifier

amplifier an electrical device which is used to make sounds louder

bellows an air-tight pouch which forces air into an instrument when it is squeezed

bones a pair of flat sticks which the player clicks together. They can be made of real bone or wood

bow a curved stick with hair stretched along its length which is used to play some string instruments

electric an instrument which makes its own sound but which must be played through an amplifier to be loud enough to hear properly

folk dance traditional dances which are danced for enjoyment or in performance

frets thin metal rods on the neck of a stringed instrument which the strings are pressed onto to change the notes

hammers sticks used for playing the dulcimer and certain percussion instruments

keys small levers on a musical instrument which the player presses to change the notes

microphone a device which picks up sounds and sends them along a wire to an amplifier

mouthpiece the part of a wind instrument which the player blows into

neck a long piece of wood on a stringed instrument which the strings are stretched along

notes musical sounds

percussion instruments which are played by hitting or shaking

plectrum a small triangular piece of plastic which is used for playing some stringed instruments

pottery clay which has been made hard by baking it in an oven

reeds thin strips of metal or cane which make a sound when air is blown across them

rosin a sticky substance which is put onto the hair of a bow to make it rub the strings of a stringed instrument

solo one musician singing or playing

washboard a flat wooden board with a bumpy surface made of metal or glass which used to be used for rubbing clothes on when they were being washed. Some are now made especially for use as instruments

FURTHER READING

Live Music! Elizabeth Sharma. Wayland, 1992

You may need help to read these other titles on music.

Eyewitness Kit: Music. Dorling Kindersley, 1993

How the World Makes Music. Iwo Zaluski and Pamela Zaluski. Young Library, 1994

The World of Music: With CD. Nicola Barber and Mary Mure. Evans Brothers, 1994

INDEX